COACH HOUSE BOOKS, TORONTO

JEN CURRIN

SCHOOL

Published with the generous assistance of the Canada Council for the Arts
and the Ontario Arts Council. Coach House Books also gratefully ac-
knowledges the support of the Government of Canada through the Canada
Book Fund and the Government of Ontario through the Ontario Book
Publishing Tax Credit.

LIBRARY AND ARCHIVES CANADA CATALOGUING IN PUBLICATION

Currin, Jen, 1972–, author
        School / Jen Currin.

Poems.
Issued in print and electronic formats.
ISBN 978-1-55245-289-9 (pbk.) / ISBN 978-1-77056-377-3 (epub)

I. Title.

PS8605.U77S34 2014   C811'.6   C2013-907681-6

Purchase of the print version of this book entitles you to a free digital copy.
To claim your ebook, please email sales@chbooks.com with proof of pur-
chase or visit chbooks.com/digital. (Coach House Books reserves the right
to terminate the free digital download offer at any time.)

For all students and seekers

'I confess that there is nothing to teach.'

— *Lao Tzu*

TABLE OF CONTENTS

THE CONDITIONS

Other people are not just relationships.

It's morning and the sun is setting.

Maybe you made the librarian look bad.

Clean the dust from your shrine.

'Cheerfully accept these conditions, determined by your past lives.'

My plants suffer in the winter.

Maybe they keep the café door open so the customers will get cold
and buy more coffee or leave.

We have all tried to keep someone/something alive.

Someone is leaving; someone is left.

Not the end of the world, just the end of *a* world.

I spent ten minutes crouched in a bookroom with my students,
listening to the computerized 'armed assailant' warning play over
and over.

After that, I was less afraid.

We are both changing and we can't change that.

What you are washing is just a body.

What I am mourning is just this.

Before we were born, you asked me.

You asked me and I said yes.

SHRINE FOR EVERY PART OF YOU

In discord

We can't be any other way

To break out of this house
you have to first break in

The holy ash scattered on the floor

Imagine a good argument

Now imagine the deepest blue of peace

In absence, waiting all day for night

In a cabinet with six farewell letters
In an oceanic bathtub
To wail over coins
To heal with water and sleep

Sympathetically
in our separate rooms
with forested bodies
and an eagerness for silence

INCREASINGLY

The owls in my night class want to believe.

If your parents were missionaries – okay.

If you are a missionary – what the fuck
are you talking about?

We all want someone to release us.
It's too painful
in this cage.

Stealing into a festooned graveyard
to steal you a ribbon –

Fathers die, friend. I don't know
what else to tell you.

And the talking cure isn't really.

I shrink away in my shoddy acts of gender.

To enter another disappointment
stale with the first kiss.

A PAIR OF SHOES

Afternoons we can mime the ditches
and die almost human.
Die hungry, having tasted night.

You're gorgeous and blunt,
telling me to wash my face.

It comes in through every window
like the words buzzing when we're alone.

Nothing is unquestionable.

Sharp pencils and careful study
when we sense something's breaking.

We could all be suddenly honest.
We could all surprise.

That careful other silence.

The death of a mother before we could ever hope
to understand her.

I hear you singing underneath your blanket
and it's so cold out this morning.

Yes, that is blood you taste.
The ever-growing space between us.

It's good to be judged, to know
how it feels.

I can give god to you, and you can give
god back to me.

We take so much medicine
but in the end it's the same amount of glass.

The illness eats away our lives in just a day or two.

I lost you after class, in the weeds and crushed water bottles.

Trying to be possibly human,
to feel pretty good about the disadvantages.

You asked the question, so I'm going to trust
that you want answers.

It's true: I accidentally ate chocolate, planned a wedding
and described an old man's perfume.

So many cloves in the chai it made my lips burn.

It's true: Woke in the pre-dawn, before bells,
excited to meditate.

True: She would have most certainly hurt me had I stayed.

HALF-LIFE

Wearing a shirt that's yours, and a tie you tied.

The schools have closed.
It's our opportunity to sleep.

Paint the bathroom, the kitchen – blue.
Egg nestled at the bottom of a huge nest.

There's no trouble to listen to, and no,
there are no vegetables in sugar.

Yet late yesterday, I ate one, and stayed home to make a mixed tape.

We have beliefs, like anyone.

We made the choices that led to these results.

Sometimes sleeping in holes dug in the ground,
sometimes in bombed-out buildings.

Accused of being optimists,
we did a lot of thinking and hesitating,
every day finding more to give away.

The same nostril kept bleeding,
but the other was clear, and through it

I could breathe.

A WEEK OF SILENCE

This is where our narratives diverge.

You went down that dry riverbed.

I climbed to the mountains.

Some say monks hide there

and that their clothes are ugly.

I found the spring and washed my face, feet and hands.

A deer with the eyes of my kindest sister

stopped near me.

All my advice fell like brittle leaves in a dying forest.

I had never felt less alone.

The green glow of ferns and nettle, water droplets on moss.

I do not wish to keep anyone

from their scheduled visit to the underworld.

So please, friend, continue on without me.

ONE VIRTUE

Boys could be in any park kissing.

The crows call them boys, anyway.

A few people are still listing reasons.

A few are choking on blackberries.

I'm a mother, son, lawyer, etc.

But we don't have anything in common.

The crows: curious, demanding.

Some mother is always there, knowing what we didn't have.

Some romances are conducted by email and some after death.

We'll be aged, polishing our bruises, calling it passion or confusion.

In the park, near the tracks ...

Just as a mirror falls and

we must work in pairs

and alone.

THE INCENSE OF THOSE ROOMS

I back away slowly.

Depending on what my needs are.

Depending on who asks.

A landscape of musk –

Selling my mask
to a cynical child.

We used to go there before the fire.

It's hard to know how to story things,
what anything means or meant.

The good of a few drops of peppermint oil.

Old betrayals burning in the back.

Aboard, I was well-read, an unreal self.

Evaluated and humiliated,

enduring
to make way for real knowledge.

It overwhelms.

'A million scarves,' is what
I wanted to say.

BACK TO OUR BODIES

I still smell like the incense of those rooms.

Come back and I will sing for you and show you I am not surprised
by death.

A ghost is made when someone dies and feels restless.

She is living in the park with a guitar.

She is one of the critics who most believes.

The city is full of verbs and selfish people.

A quiet class of city dwellers siphoning all the money.

Hovering above their habitual clinics, I saw the sickness and paranoia,

the waves of fatherly protectiveness,

the cold intelligence animating it all.

And I fell.

The unthinkable happens.
And then what? Then what do you think?

If the monks meant it
at our hospice
we will meditate.

Consciousness has become big business —
and our expectations were unreasonably high.

A small moment on Starbird Road:
You kissed my forehead
and I saw things differently.

What should I say to her now?
She is just a stranger.

The music is painful, intentional.

We get angry and try to reject the photographer.

She killed a morning with her shattered glass,
her essay smelling of cigarettes.

We didn't know how impatient
it all could be.

Sleeping in the cold, making fiction with our eyes.

Everything in place
as we are moved.

WEIRD SHRINE

We don't know the names of the streets.

We bike down.
We bike down.

Zero family members are travelling with me.

I bike down.

Sleep-deprived-like, ferry wind & ice cream
if you ask.

We took it all seriously & personally.
We took a lot of pills.
We killed a lot of mothers
in our dreams
& we hid a lot of little boys in baskets.

We are not like my heaven.

& we are biking down.

A horned deer-child, bird-like, gnawing the dictionary binding.

Your myriad forms.

Your breath smells like bananas,
but you are not a baby.

Here we are again, in the presence of a living saint.

What, no questions to ask?

No dances, then?

No heaven?

Dear, I am a young man.

Dear, absent-mindedly I …

Take my lives, take these lines.

Dear, residents will know how inconvenient …

Dear, remember the night bus, how we fell in & out of caffeine?

Jingling with the music you purchased from the clouds.

An astronaut you called your father.

How nonsense always made sense.

That scholar of fairy tales.

We were nodding-reading. Swimming-fucking. & lying-believing.

How simple it was until we had to finally forget ourselves.

Right down to what we were drinking & wearing.

My lips peeling. I had no feelings.

Disentangling, dear, & so many more people to befriend …

Where will I put this list?

I can love another face once I learn how.

These are my remedies; these are my addictions.

Barely doing my job.

You are breezing through, grabbing bread,

hemming a dress & sucking a lemon:

'I need your chequebook & your clothes.'

Words to utter as I compose heaven: 'Damn you, thank you.'

One January I walked in the woods at night.

In a clearing, I saw an owl.

After that, I became honest.

Haven't had a cold or a headache since.

When your eyes meet mine

don't forget the vulnerability of that open space.

FRIENDSHIPS (UNLIKELY)

I wrote this dream to address the problem.

The problem was my dreams.

I am responsible for the fantasy –

just as I knowingly paid for coffee with a counterfeit twenty.

Another friend is 'glowing.'

'The wind is kind.' (*She* said?)

After giving up everything –

how blue the sky.

Clean hopelessness –

not getting anything from anyone else. (A lie.)

She was testing/teasing/teaching me –

like the men joking about feasting on grain-fed pigeons.

He was both fat & rich in the parable,

single-handedly keeping the patriarchy alive.

Asking & asking what to do.

She reminded me that I could write stories,

could be struck by lightning & live.

LOSS ORIENTATION

Here's one theory of grief:

'I'm a simple person, a lake,' my friend said.

'I am a thinking, eating machine,' said my other friend.

The photo of a dead husband travels with him.

At night, lying in bed, he remembers he is not

his body & wonders what will be left when he dies.

He sleeps on his stomach & dreams of perfume.

In the morning, he writes a letter to his dead husband.

The trunk packed, the cabinets empty, the light

falling all over his face –

ANTI-DEPENDENT

How is life different after death?

There is so much of yourself you don't know.

The smell of grilled peppers coming down the fire escape.

Some students will never speak – just accept that.

I heard you took a cow's life.

I heard you cut yourself.

There are different, scary voices –

cats who can read your mind

& doorways of trust/distrust.

Meaning a student calls down the hall –

wants to make you dinner, says you smell

of old bad tea.

Your way of going about things

has brought & is going to bring suffering.

If you had scissors right now.

If you read another book about shape-shifters.

If you knew what sleep was exactly.

How often I have looked for a war

& found only this –

'I'd rather be naked,' my friend said
as we kissed in the snow.

She crashed into me, we fell & made a very strange angel.

I don't hear anything unzipping & I don't want to.

This dynamic present as I catch the wrong bus *again*.

A bridge to nowhere ...

Enter our sexual conversations.

At the incense parlour, I bought you a box & some sticks.

Pulling back in a 'public' space.

You apologize for interrupting me, then interrupt again.

Don't seem to understand that my erotic beauty
does not depend on you, or anyone.

The path shows up in dreams as abandoned railroad tracks.

An owl might be in a tree listening.

& you might be blond then, in a light summer dress,
strolling distractedly, weeds dangling from your hands.

Friend, when will you really inquire?

I can't – I don't want to – acquire you.

Light the incense & watch the smoke disappear.

What I have to offer: sex & friendship,

a sea of tension.

You poke my belly & my back.

Am I pregnant again?

With you.

Retrieving, waiting … your name rhymes with 'bliss.'

You refuse to read the poet in translation

even if there is a story about babies carrying all the knowledge inside.

o

Now I'm turned on by your notebook doodles.

What is this?

Years of self-study & values & sunken, worried flesh

& we still want

to cure the disorder ourselves.

Let's talk about water while drinking water.

Suddenly we can understand everything our teachers were saying.-

FRAGMENTED LESSON PLAN

Yes, we took walks.

& we were just getting to know each other sexually.

Soy milk separates from coffee.

I have an anxiety.

An ability to quickly give up hope.

Everybody was busy loving the fracture.

A trick: Let her have her way.

We became ants in the garden: Seven lives ago.

& then I slept on the floor in a room with laughter in it.

At some point you will be who you say you are.

Not in spite of, but because of.

The children gave us blue & green marbles & told us to visit again.

It was a special kind of poverty we had to work very hard to win.

At his old school, he was afraid of friends.

& we covered up the love bites with turtlenecks & went to teach.

Detrimental swoop, buzz & stomp.

Be my ground; now fly.

I've breezed through eloquence: I'm on to blunt death.

The devices of torture – I'm talking about the mind here.

You're afraid, I'm afraid, we took a baguette

into the sex shop & now we're eating lunch

with the cashier who is also a cat

stretching in the slice of sun under the window.

Where is our paddle?

Where is our boat?

Dreams of you in floral dresses & high boots.

They were lonely sandwiches, the ones we ate.

In order of importance, please list your sex toys.

It's like the time the student came to my office

to discuss literary terms & pussy willows

& I had to keep what they call a straight face.

But what are *your* defences?

Mine are just beginning.

SEAWEED & CRANBERRY JUICE

Goddammit, I want a blood test & a colonic,

the keys to your mouldy apartment,

a hat or a haircut, carbohydrates

like a pregnancy.

You listen to two waters – one is whispering,

'A vegan will kill me.'

Seagulls reel outside your apartment.

Did you leave enough space for loneliness?

'Only straight people use the word *partner* now,' my friend informed
    me.

You'll make a nice dinner & set it by the dumpster.

Swing by with your cloth shopping bag full of egg cartons
    & intentions,

possessions to drink as the moon roars.

My undergraduate friend described what it was like

her first time on heroin: 'Everything perfect.

Placing a glass down on the table –

the most perfect thing.' I felt it

years later, completely sober, slightly caffeinated,

watching a red leaf fall from a tree.

THE AUDITION

Your friend shoved her knife

into your chest.

A bee outside your head

was telling you to leave your body.

You had memorized no one's number,

had looked & acted too sober.

Now you fall over, suddenly – an image of yourself

sweeping a burning house

rises.

o

An awful awe.

So calm.

What to come.

o

Through blood, through fire, through tea-stained robes.

Through the cigarettes you gave up last week,

the most beloved wrinkles at the corners of your eyes –

& Guan Yin's merciful hands

on the broom.

o

Through the mists, an ally, smoking in the alley.

What will she look like & what will she be capable of saying?

She smiles, she cleans her dusty knife,

pulls a baguette from her backpack & slices it.

Where is the cheese? The apples? The moon?

You meet an ally in an alley & she doesn't stab you to death.

Not this time.

IN THE VILLAGE OR PRAY ALONE

What is a lasting friendship?

No one really knows.

I didn't want to disappoint them,

purposely chose negative, elusive people.

But every time she insisted, I became less amused, more restless.

Let her play her karma out while I signal joy & sip dandelions.

Twisting versions of our experiences –

The phone rang three times; I couldn't recognize myself.

Concentrating my doubts: writing another saint paper.

Entangled in stupid questions, we learned to be more serene.

Weary or just withdrawn, listening to magnetic appeals

& calling for a prayer

to increase our bewilderment.

Just another hour in your fantasy book.

Tattered host, will you make a friend on the train?

A reversal of lives, living in this damaged community.

Good deeds are never wasted. (Wrote the student.)

Wondering why we trip & fall.

What we learn.

This subject does not interest because ...

This infatuation ...

All this information ...

The central library is the only place we can find these.

The day I danced, hiked, swam.

All of these ugly books.

Very little time, & no privacy.

A city girl, afraid of trees.

When our parents were on vacation.

Waking in pain in the middle of the night.

You never said you understood, & all these years later,

I don't know if you *did* understand.

There were things we all forgot to do.

Like love.

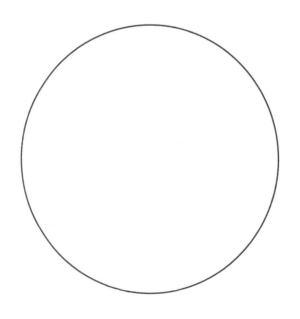

MAKE HASTE

The beginning will be imagined.

After that we'll sleep & eat.

I could be coming home from California right now.

You could be dozing in the grass.

Our room is harmless in terms of karma.

But the smoke is endless.

You're on a leash; I'm the dog.

What we know of music is sound –

sound with the quality of touch.

A horrible state: pretending to love one another.

These relationships always start with lies &

you can guess where they go from there.

Let's put these keys in the sink & wash them.

There is one key that isn't marked.

That's the one to keep.

MUSEUM OF GLASS

Two children took the black clock outside,

smashed it to pieces with a rock.

I had wondered about the song.

Wondered & wondered –

then started to sing along.

Combing crumbs from the pages –

can you make out the words?

It's too hot here to miss you, or anyone.

Everyone's steamed glasses,

a fly who shares my coffee.

In some circumstances there is nothing better than sleep deprivation.

The anarchist bookstore is open every day from 12–8. Sometimes.

New food, new fantasy –

more responsibility.

I remember opening a window, but not which one.

Spice rags. What we pick up is amaranth.

I've been washing & washing.

Watching & watching.

'Heaven knows … ' someone started to say.

But what is heaven? & what does it know?

There are eggshells, there is an eggshell sky, a book half-finished,

a student shooting her last roll of film.

Even she wants to write

a hopeful story, though she can't/doesn't know how.

The street is already sewn back up & the watches

are feeling beautiful & grateful.

So closely we heal that we can't decide: starve, or fast?

For charm

a bracelet is needed, & the range of a good mood.

I woke up Sunday with 500 words & no desire.

How to stay in my body when feeling joy

was the question

the healer never asked me.

It's like asking why you're afraid

of darkness

but not the dark.

Because I've been walking.

Because I have no devices.

Because you said without artifice.

This blood dying on my fingernail –

& we will get married in a grove of magnolias.

Those years – it was pretty healthy – a west coast

way of talking – question marks at the end of every sentence –

I could feel it in the coffee & in the dreams.

There are all kinds of battles: tiny little mountains

& tall possibilities.

You consult with a dead bug & a happy baby.

You take everything made & unmake it.

I'd rather be walking for three hours.

If I have a bike, I have to worry about locking it.

If I have a suitcase, I have to carry it.

What we do without question is what we do to others is why we are
  not disturbed enough & disturb the other passengers.

So as to be marked.

So as to smack.

Elastic & honest: we are the same

person slowly sipping a curse –

most strong, most dangerous of teas.

THE MOULD DOCTOR

Moody, the office
is raw garlic & cayenne water –
all the ginger tea we got married to
& now disorder, unaccustomed as we are
to harmony.

She brought chaos,
enrolled in sniper school.
Spinning, spinning, & controlled drinking –
the very life, the very poverty.
Just normal agitation. It's quite simple, really.
Six months of breast
or soy milk & a tiny cracked ring
we threw in the ocean.
Example: You hire someone to commit a crime.
Example: You live next to the highest light.
There will be two kinds of water – no, more.
One kind will bring us to the bird sanctuary
with no bread crumbs & no kindness.
It's quite simple, really.
What you called an education was just mould.
& now my lungs ache & there is a rash on my face.
Today you are counting my breaths
as I commit the crime of breathing.

It was cold. I hoped someone would read a manifesto or hold my hand.

We always lied the same lie.

At the same time, we were ambiguous about our identities.

I had a spirit in my stomach & you had red slippers.

There were headache medications we could buy.

'All I remember is that she gave me homework.'

'Who?'

'You!'

But I don't remember what it was.

She drifted into sleep & woke to a friendship, sucking ice cubes in the bath.

'So this is life outside the hospital.'

Vague in both cases, yet the same: 'Me, mine, my idea.'

Who am I but just another teacher with too many little pencils?

I see a claw mark on your cheek & an exam booklet in your hand.

It's another story about a girl & the woods.

ATTENDING COLLAGE

We cut naked pictures out of magazines.

Casually brutal – 'I'm going to explore that … '

Her strength comes from living in a tent in all seasons.

An illusion we had to heal.

'All this food is clogging my style.'

We attended late classes. We cut class
& went to the beach.

Cut paper dolls out of the syllabus.

Paper dolls in pants – perfect for the fire.

So solstice came with its non-moon & saw us fishing –
for something.

'Do you feel like you chose her?' my brother asked.

She's write

& I don't ever understand.

Until yes, yes

I do.

THE WHOLE WIND

Someone at a party told me Mercury was in retrograde
& then asked how I found my poems.

Later he read a list of vulnerabilities &
we all held hands.

The children always steal spoons & listen to the dogs –

I can just barely bandage the past
enough for them to believe to go on.

It's early morning & the I Ching is not promising.

Tribes/tribal/hive-mind: the old way of loving.

A relentless tallying, a keeping track –
& calling this relationship.

I ate something selfish yesterday & now feel sick.

The whole house smells like mouldy dirt,
the curtain rod whipped off by the wind –

In my bare feet.

The sidewalk.

I'm knowing you now.

Send someone.

Send.

(I like to breathe.)

There are essentials & there is essential.

Apple tree, police, paper dolls – just ordinary gaps.

Pretty soon we will make idiots of our thoughts.

Measure the fragments, change our clothes, spread a few rumours.

This is something like a lie

but I want to hear it:

the flowering viewing, the belief that we have different problems.

Babies outlive our teeth –

just another godly detail

as we begin this unfinishable work.

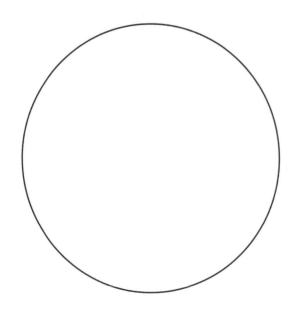

THE HOUSE CHOIRS

She pours out everything she remembers,
the red trees & the forest.

One day, she showed me a list of all the doctors available.
She brought two spoons to my house & told me to eat.

'Why shouldn't we experience this?'
I shouted to the blazing house.

The babies were already talking & walking.

The important issue was:
we were not an academic institution.

There was a joke we heard & a story we liked.
But in the end it became his lecture
& we weakly repeated, 'How? Why?'

A week later she called me: 'Look out the window. It's windy.'

And I'm lonely, lonely as I sift
through the dissatisfying clothes
of my father's depression.

'When the words come out, they will be certain,' she reminded.

I'd like to believe this could be a new conversation,
Father taking his dolls out
of the closet-box & telling one last story.

A teenager called to his authentic self.

The soldiers in the dresser drawer finally falling asleep.

As I return to my volunteer job of cleaning bones with a toothbrush
& she performs her early winter exercises,
they rope off the scary area.

He repeats his story a thousand times.

We will not obtain troops, but we will stand
with our sisters, our brothers, their families, & their families' families . . .

(We all will.)

AFTER STREET & AFTER SHIVER

My sister said, 'People! People!'
Not 'women,' not 'men.'
But you didn't hear –

No loner bound …
No longer bored …

Went through & deleted the messages
then pictures

& buzzed around the apartment.

She says the garden will have to give.

We are being kicked out again.

It used to be a place we slept
to forget our bodies.

A discarded sink deep with prayer.

A place to wash out our socks
& turn on the critical schools.

Study lyric in garbage cans,
loot the library.

It's local and needs your help. It's
utopic & bleeds like a head.

THE EMERGENCIES

There was this woman in the store who said hi.

'Hello,' I said. & then I realized

she was a ghost.

Before I have to run, one last question:

is Virginia still in Texas?

I beg of you. Be silent with me.

We will need this skill, depending on the nature of the emergency.

I have always wanted to make a beautiful gesture.

To be a mother but not give birth.

Forbear/forbearance: two passports in my back pocket.

Spiritually harmless, this handwriting, this error-&-trial process.

Up the trail: goats & the cabins for sleeping.

The children on guitars, long-haired children with bright sad faces.

Children with dandelion beards & things to say.

We must listen.

They will have it harder than us.

Now that the winds, the fires have begun.

The shaking. The shock.

A ROOF

I once held a white moth in my hands.

An oral friend called to please me.

We were lighter after the war.

I mean we were nearly starved.

Hating trains, hating Father's Day ...

There were curtains there. I couldn't do
what 'I wanted to.'

A neighbour stalked the street, practicing his punches.

The country below us had already started to steal
water for its military crops.

The deserts bloomed.

We read about salmon & became emotional.

Events & people disagree on this subject

but the difficult ones are with us
as we build these temporary shelters.

Our faces lit by candlelight ...

The accordions mournful ...

A scene of power & disappointment: the end.

ON A CLOUD

Phone the doctor-spirit. She has healed millions
& will curse this vehicle
to death.

There are many people in the womb
when they bomb us.

It's a symbolic fever, like possible love.

What we smell is trivial, noticing
the awe of a ghost.

Just remember how the story goes: 'I don't want to hear ... '

The huge toxic water & the shivering fish.

A friend's fight with linear time.

Iodine tablets under our tongues, eyes radiating –

No matter how complex the structure

when it melts
we float.

& the ghost-doctor demands an answer,
paddling towards her dream –

THE OCEANS

The work has been done, now will you just be honest about it?

You're at home applying for an artist's grant

& I'm making sauerkraut with six friends.

'I feel your seaweed body bending my way.'

Is that what you said?

Or was it the crying yoga teacher

talking about cancer & revolution?

She's still out biking in the sun,

hamburgers after chemo & much laughter.

When a nuclear plant is destabilized, we taste it

in every neighbourhood, hear it

ringing in our ears.

I want to hold my friends who survived

the debris of that tall city

& tell them not to worry

but we are all worried

as another wave looms.

'The fact is, we live in a city, & cities are busy,'

the yoga teacher explained. 'I did an experiment.

One day I smiled at everyone on the bike path &

the next day I frowned.'

It was after a movie about an earthquake,

what it did to seaweed & families.

To someone's wind coming across a body.

You enjoyed stimulants & taught them English for a while

before they moved back

& started shaking. They taught you

how to look up at the luminescent trees,

how to take a leaf, tear it

& make a wish.

WE ARE THE 100%

Yes, I am A Friend Of The Environment.

Poverty decides, sometimes.

Impossible sometimes.

Waking & wrecking the little decorations she gave me

for my borrowed green apartment.

I am the custodian, the grandpa, the all-the-rage

garden restaurant, & I'm very tired, with the fatigue

of something like a choice,

but not feeling so free, relapsing –

'I would like to think of her with mercy,' I said.

'Then do it,' he said. 'Just think of her with mercy.'

Is it because? Because of any of these?

'This guy just started to cut my hair. That's how I got a haircut.'

I wanted to see what the system would look like in crisis.

I wanted to be more honest.

This much mental suffering shouldn't go to waste.

Come to our party. Come early. Intuit what we most need.

IMPERFECT TEACHERS

It's during chemo, & obviously, you're tired.

We don't want to share these bodies with just anyone.

But I can feel warmth from our last meeting

so it probably won't be as painful as before.

Let's make some meaning & recall it as a joyful scene.

An open god-path: finally the moon shines into the forest.

To explain togetherness, I will use the analogy of fruits & vegetables.

It was dark in the woods like eggplant & plum,
a certain kind of veined kale.

Her generous acts – now vagaries – weren't really.

The things we do for others that we're really doing for ourselves.

Being visible & visiting people when we'd rather just hide & die.

At least we got halfway there, shared our notebooks
& talked chance procedures.

A way to be close to the drunk father: get drunker.

To the dead father: play dead.

I have come early to watch this disastrous show

& I am taking notes – using first person, it's convenient – taking this
barely ready body to the beach

& there we will light the discourses.

Yes, after all this, we have finally

discovered fire.

PHOTO BOOTH

I've given up thinking about you in a sexual way.

It's boring to me now.

& the view from the camera ...

The view from the imaginary phone booth ...

I understand the owl to be winking at me.

Drop a stone in the next water & pray

for what I can't forgive – snow

with little infinity.

No flies, no files, no dark feelings – is this you?

I don't think I'm ugly, but I'm definitely

the ugliest one in this group.

Just as a headache drills through the wall &

people speak delightfully, archly.

Stubbornness can be exciting – for a while.

But then it gives way to boredom. & after boredom – freedom.

You're a descriptive kind of girl.

In your childhood, strange women spoke in tongues

& since then you've had issues with syntax.

Unveil the fathers: in black suits, into black magic.

Such fury to keep this poison-system afloat.

Before we get a response from them,

we should ask ourselves:

What is that air in my head?

Have I really been listening?

I woke up so slowly, friend. It was like

midnight had given me

pictures of all the answers

& now I had to sort through them.

TAKING AN INTUITION CLASS

Those old hippies in the picture aren't

my parents; they're my friends

& I hope you give back those library books

you stole in Arizona & right the rusted

sign on your neighbour's front lawn.

Yes, she gave a few pears years ago & promised

a sort of friendship, a boat we could all

escape in when the waters rose.

But we weren't so easily cooled.

There was a dance in the firehall & a desire for crawling.

A child just learning to open a book & point at the words.

There were pictures to help us understand how it would unfold &
    what to do.

The first illustration was about clinging.

The second told a story of the plastic island in the ocean.

After that we closed the book & took a few breaths.

Out back blackberries are ripening

& in this room we can

work in practical & mysterious ways.

Unterrible & terribly inefficient, we make

a noise, we message a house.

We understand a little. Just a little of us.

W.A.I.T.: WHY AM I TALKING?

Moving? No, I am not
so easily moved.

Red is red is mystery is red.

What?

What is the mystery?

Dating some mystic you met online,
cleaning her teeth & shining her vehicle.

Why do her kindnesses taste like hate mail?

The little backless benches in museums – made for getting it on –
are where we slept in guards' uniforms.

How weird it is to see *SELF* in big neon letters
& *STORAGE* next to it.

I worry that I made the wrong mistake.

That there was another, more fruitful, mistake I should have made.

This is the magic of a bee or a fly.

We, the other people, whine & pour
glasses of it into empty bodies.

It's just somewhere we stopped, on the street, near the community
gardens, to continue our deep green conversations.

Bliss is not teaching

& love is

not

an exchange.

(Ex change.)

(Change.)

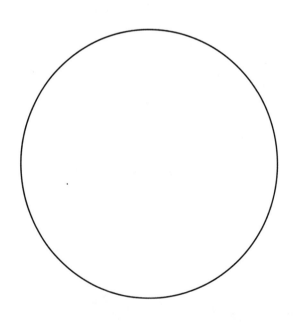

You moved across the country to live in my studio.

You are my twin.

We have access to all these schools & all these empty classrooms.

Something your phone stuttered –

but I don't text at breakfast.

& that's how I spent last summer: lonely.

My relations used our meetings as opportunities to drink.

My thoughts rusted like old coins in a living fountain.

Just to get coherent –

to give up our feelings for these machines.

The women of Denver were so generous.

At a party one gave me a silver ring.

Another time, an acquaintance slipped me her shoes

& walked home barefoot.

I have no idea who is a woman

& who isn't & no interest

in pursuing the question.

We're all mothers & we're all death

& at 18 we had fake IDs, decisions

made out of fear & snow –

The lying is in us still.

I don't know when it went walking

& when it returned.

We always miss at least one quarter of the movie for some reason.

We'd rather read the acknowledgements than the book itself.

We don't want to encourage this smell.

The crows cawing across the city are us.

Between fight & flight: awkward reading.

Yesterday I saw beehives & a phone on the ground.

Because we didn't believe in the possibilities of gelatinous relationship.

Deciding things/this side of things.

'I just want to be really committed.'

In no way is it your personality/history/foggy mornings before the
 sun burns off.

'The classrooms are set up this way, so we teach this way.'

A big peace is coming – & what will it look like?

Underneath everything a laughter so contagious

it won't let us sit still.

My nose is pierced in the afterlife

across the sea

& I am very committed,

two glasses of water

on a table set for one.

They were children first, & rainy,

releasing everything in themselves

except this intimacy, this anchor.

On the counter, decanted water.

We have this idea of pain & the idea itself brings pain.

Things so suddenly shift – I often get intentionally lost.

We'll be up early, coming home on the ferry.

Butterfly, speak to me. Or snake.

When we wake up how much is it going to hurt.

These are cold spring days. In your yellow room

I wasted three hours

& called it 'lovemaking.'

It wasn't even sex – just a boring shipwreck

bumping the ocean floor.

But I know when I look in someone's eyes

& they are with me.

Two lanterns on a dark mountain road.

FOR THE DIRECTIONS

Almost as beautiful as a blond woman with a dark moustache.

An uncomfortable act, perfect today.

Broken lights on the bus & a girl's violence –

all the people she wants to punch in the face.

I called my spiritual family close.

Today we would turn to theatre.

The nephew in swimming goggles & grandmother

with lips of glass.

We're just playing a role, but it's very sincere.

We pucker up & listen.

No idea where we are, but the two-year-old's impeccable syntax

calms us.

'My name is Beauty. Rose. Empty,' he says.

THE BEACH ELECTRIC

Having nothing better to do than make pigeons fat –
Concerned with emotional contagion –
Can't bring herself to move with anything like hurry –

'I didn't have that kind of mother. I was free.'
We sipped under those trees two summers ago.
He/she/they were beautiful/gentle/drunk.

It's not as easy as throwing a brick
through a window & asking
the question, 'Who will stay in New York?'

She's just two hospitals away. In April,
kissing an acknowledgements page, a very long one.

Another part of 'us' 'you' can't see.

The soundness of a sleep – our position
'has been made redundant.'

Coffee spilled on a notebook, an instant map.
Possibilities of a city. The thought of being
left out, another only child Gemini
with sand-encrusted toes & a jar of sea glass.

On the bus he asks her, 'What kind
of porn do you like? What kind? Tell me!'

& she finally whispers, 'Lesbian.'

'Not men?'

'What?'

'*Men*. Not men?'

Quiet laughter. 'No.'

Before, we wrote many mistakes.

Now, we hesitate. & write more mistakes.

Saturday: strangely satisfied by her incomplete
narrative, I got up & stretched.
Three days/six orgasms later
we were friends again.

THE UNFAMILIAR GLOVES

Wary, every body, every vision,

everywhere we rushed with our urgent dissolving problems.

Walking home from meditation I heard an accordion.

Saw *love* spray-painted on a fence in red

& next to it, in black, DIE, &

I thought I saw you walking in the park.

It was so long ago, when breakfast was coffee, cigarettes & fatigue.

Moodily waiting for instructions & keeping

ourselves busy with gossip.

The loud hush of sex in a small room,

sharp blue midnight, friends gathering around

the firepit in your backyard &

your haircut grew out girlish.

We do this thing – it's called conversation.

It's called playing 'spiritual counsellor.'

It's called a space we once entered together.

After a month I left the hospital & returned to the library

where I shelved hundreds of self-help books

& read none of them.

THE REAL

We are moments of two beings.

We are beings of movement.

Responsible & animal.

It's people like us who animate this fantasy,

so fired up.

It's morning & I'm jasmine green caffeinated

& so annoyed

to be one of them.

People attaching monarch wings to their backs –

up on the roof, saying they can fly.

I am just a fly.

The buzzing never stops.

Mistake the role or take the role.

We could be more careful/careless/phoneless/carless.

We could paint/taste the pleasures/mimic the teachers.

It's all *poof!*

Beings in a building – we are destined

to be dried-up rivers.

The way my voice enters a leaf as it crumbles.

FAIRY & SICK

It was after I accidentally dropped my computer

down a sewer grate –

You had just sent me an email:

'A friend in the U.S. Everyone needs one.'

One woman's fatigue is another's energy –

a portfolio of circular images & strange wind.

Like the smell of fall blackberry bushes.

Everything is suddenly night in your stories –

but I want to annihilate the distances between us.

Give up this texting relationship

& actually answer the phone.

I'm sorry, but I'm just not sentimental about death.

Mine, yours, anyone's.

Your father said he was 'going home'

& my grandmother asked the nurse

to open the window just another inch.

GREEN WHISTLE

Everyone knows the answer

& the questions they can guess.

I don't want to live

with my beloved

this wet week.

She said, 'Stomp stomp, be a woman about it.'

Stay calm as the fig tree

is dying & I'll comb my cat.

But what kind of cushion is that?

There's a story she started to tell

three times & never finished.

A silverfish swimming in my writing notebook.

If you don't think about it too much, you'll learn.

Hear it now or later – when

it seems like anything could be a joke.

Those great holy castles, flu-induced

states of surrealism –

After the sickness we change the sheets

& at the grocery I hear two lovers

talking about end times & kale.

ALL THE MYSTERIES

Two foxes, two figs,

a glass of sparkling water,

a quaking bed.

Someone learns her theory by heart from a hypocrite

& now performs in cold red slippers.

Slipping into a hot bath sprinkled with spearmint,

I have prayed to lose you,

kissing near-sleep with something like honesty.

All the masters in their long robes floating

at the windows.

'Rose, rose, rose,' you laughed,

twirling down the tree,

& let go of my hand.

She told me to call her the next time my tongue turned black.

This is romance.

A bed in a dying room.

A city gasping.

Is it poverty that makes us so self-promoting?

Pillows piled on top of each other like bodies.

To hate romance & seem

to call everything your body –

in the night we can do surprising things.

Jog in the fog, sing radio.

As soon as I saw someone's shame –

we're incompatible, right?

The whole relationship happened in bed one night.

We committed to this TV show

starring flies, dead bees & the future.

To love romance, what sugar burns to say,

vibrating like a phone in a front pocket.

You are in the same position –

the tea smell, the empty library & the cold, cold air.

It was after days of medicine.

We were very high those weeks in the woods.

Our biographies bleeding, hung on a line to dry.

I will never give a talk again.

My motives so suspect.

If only the words could come out of another mouth.

In meditation, our legs disappeared.

One volunteered to give a talk on cars,

the sound of them swishing in the rain.

'What will you talk on?' the teacher asked me &

I felt despair. I wished I could bring

myself to like a book as much as the mountains.

My friend the poetic twinkled an idea.

But I wasn't having it, wrapping

myself in another itchy personality.

'We will walk, not drive, to the funeral,' the teacher said.

I hoped it would rain & that someone would

break the silence with oranges.

On the road, neighbours leave bowls

of rice & lentils, strings of dried peppers.

A saint & a sculptor thread fingers.

I have never been so sure of my life.

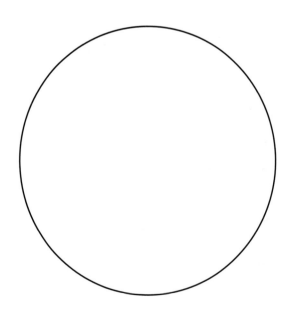

'I'm about to have a seizure,' he said,

& sat down on the train.

o

I am shaking uncontrollably,

& someone throws salt in my face.

Even our motives are at present misunderstood.

I shake & shake my head, trying to get rid of the horrible scene

& I see a bit of anxiety in your face.

'Yes, they have gone to jail with us.' A nurse embraces his mother.

'Never before have I written so long a letter.'

We met in these rooms, unrolled these papers, circled these parks.

We went dancing, studied oppression, massaged our feet, & questioned
interiority.

A sober eroticism animated the slow hours.

It kept making sense, even when nothing else did.

We met late at night, & earlier, we sat outside unfriendly buildings,
we wove baskets out of newspapers.

We finally wanted it all to make some sort of deep sense.

We wanted to live that way now

& we knew there was not one trapped person who would disagree
with us.

Already we were forgetting the former politicians & their babysitters.

We mispronounced their names & felt happy.

We had sat in their bathwater too long without ever getting clean.

o

'Define *just* and *unjust*,' he finally said, in a tone so gentle it made us weep.

FEATHERS & BLOOD

I'm another student who wants to write about the 'human condition.'

Other than that, I seem wise enough.

So quickly we become bored by the subject –

The authors, the bumpy devices –

The night defined by its silence & horrible spells.

The task for spiritual workers now –

My friend's nightmares – the full year before she married the corporate
   lawyer:

of old women eating cake in the dark. 'Or maybe it *wasn't* cake,' she said.

This same woman, sleep-deprived, once hallucinated all of Manhattan
   in flames.

From our humble offices, we appeal –

In a room of scattered logics,

objects of responsibility.

A system based on selfishness. & how we uphold it.

o

We killed him, squished his body into a bottle.

It leaked on the floor, & the children tracked bloody footprints.

Feathers blew in through the open door.

Confusing evidence for when the cops came.

I Ching: 'The spirits are certainly with you!'

The spirits are certainly.

Our task now.

Lightest footsteps like rain

healing death from our faces.

We first started to think these things in the hospital,

bound to wet beds in green-lit rooms.

At first uncertain, fingers on the light switch.

Corporate laughter echoing in the halls.

It wasn't the kind of strength we wanted.

It wasn't strong enough.

No match to strike.

No match for this unravelling.

SUITS & PEOPLE

They told us we couldn't grow our own vegetables,

could only buy prescriptions.

Our phones were poisoning us

& the oceans were dead beyond any human imagining.

We still – some say naively – believed in cooperation.

Suchness & signlessness, effort & effortlessly.

Many lacked presence: a signlessness of the times.

Yet we could flatten fences & guerrilla garden.

Share handkerchiefs & water bottles to fend off tear gas.

Yet I'm just as alive in retreat, remembering

my brother who died a cop

& came back a hurt mother.

S/he begged their father to give up

the uniform & the gun

on the street corner where you once

biked the shape of an infinity sign

forty times for a friend's birthday.

We will not give up. We will not stop burning.

My hand in yours.

'I don't know where she's from.'

Something a stupid white person might say.

Another volunteer whitens,

thinking 'doing good' is enough

on the path.

You have failed me as an ally again.

Let's get coffee.

Collect rocks. To rock your world. I

refuse to eat vegetables, to hinge

at the hips.

When you bake the cake/make the magazine,

think of me.

Another apologist like my friend

made out of paper. Eating ice cream

out of a huge freezer and hating the word *spiritual*.

We can't understand. We can, & hallucinate

out of body.

There's really nothing to observe –

these books allowed them to avoid responsibility

but even absentees eventually get lonely.

At the corner of Powell & Garden

she sharpens – I mean, files – her nails

& tells me, 'Corn is a vegetable & god

is a woman.'

The tone has/hasn't changed.

The conversation is still happening.

In September the conversation will start over again.

I might be a dean but I'm also just a person.

A person with ideas.

If there are absences.

If you were absent.

A medical note. Talk to me.

The deans meet on May 9 or 10.

To actually belong.

To find pain

even ordinary.

We are the deans of painters.

Expectedly early in the war.

The rise of the makers.

The actual dappled summer light.

Streams, trees, flesh.

We are the painter's wounds:

small, sharp, zero, original.

The conversation continues, faithful to the fathers.

The sons try to work a magic

for the glowing movie above.

It is no longer ourselves.

At a talkback we talk back.

The learning is in trying.

I've lifted the sky from my back.

They boiled the coffee

for words, for hours.

Cry, pray, howl, etc.

Just more answers I can't understand.

Someone is moving closer to death,

writing a cheque for my life.

You are telling yourself a very compelling self-saboteur story.

This song will be stuck in my head all day.

A poet on Beach Avenue, a poet on Hawks Street.

When she was a child she felt

like she didn't belong anywhere & so

keeps ruining every sense of belonging.

I will never have a husband or a dog.

& I don't work for money.

The water is full of god,

cold as my hands in these unfamiliar gloves.

Late night bike ride, thawing dawn.

What we loved for, why we bothered.

I left my wallet at the top of the hill

& coasted down.

A perfect saint dies in an automobile crash.

These are the pictures of her at one year.

Things like this happen all the time.

'Nations' are 'built'; 'good' neighbourhoods 'made.'

Gentle or harsh – I'm just going to ask you &

I only have this one language.

On our customs declaration form:

books, seaweed, tampons, tea.

We took everything from the list we made

& put it in the recycling bin.

See, I'm a different kind of scholar.

You won't find me at school.

Look for me in the weeds of the community garden,

down at the train tracks, paddling a canoe

up the canal, washing dishes in this or that kitchen,

wiping a baby's ass or braiding a sister's hair.

I've already said too much & now I'm worried I've lost you.

But I gave up worry long ago & so –

Here. This.

WEATHER & HORMONES

Interested in envelopes, what
is under clothes. Not closed –
what we danced to, hiccup
happenings. Everything grass & we rolled
around, down hills understood
as sugar, the way a hip
juts, listening to that Northwest white boy with the sweet voice.
'I am the great fires,' he kept saying.
He was younger & less dumb than us.

During that time I was trying to learn
how to write love poems, how to ignore
my self-consciousness & give up acts of negligence.
Into the literatures I fell as if into a dead sleep.

Soon money will be over & then
where will we be?
Money, please ignore me
so I may enter the deep
holiness of morning.

'When in rain … ' the white boy sang
as we collapsed in other rooms.

I told a friend there is always room for romance.
Footsteps, process, a slap & a laptop lap dance.
Just learning how to get around
like white smoke wearing
a pair of stolen white sunglasses.

You say you forgot
your magic for a while, friend.
Well okay then. Come over &
we can eat green things in silence,
let someone else hang up or answer
the phone.

My mother taught me how to answer the phone.
When someone asks to speak to you, you say, 'She's dead,' & laugh.

This will keep disaster & jealousy away.

It's 2012 & people are still getting married, still
having babies. The fertility clinics are full.

Cancer is eating a bowel, a lung, a stomach.
Countries are coughing up wars & the sculptures
of ourselves are burning with ideas.

An idea scalded me just yesterday
in the coffee shop. From the depths
of a search – shoes off – invisible –

I saw a girl with a tattoo like a splotch of dirt
on her calf. People were pouring smoke
out of their nostrils
& talking excitedly from too much caffeine.
A fellow didactic cradled his arms.

It's July, & we're still holding umbrellas.
Still fighting about gender & money.

A green moth flies into the shop & no one notices.

Our friends are tree-sitting in Oregon
or deejaying in Montreal.
We're trying out for the anarchist choir.

Some puppets are up high, some are dancing
on the ground.

Are you someone who acts too often out of obligation?

Me too.

The woman in mediation class so ardently
telling her group, 'Every day, in the shower,
I think, 'I just want
to be *free*.'

We had a great friendship while you were living.

One of the most watchable actors in the vulgar States.

Dreaming the hots for him/her.

The tenderness of emotionless of –

We occupied

& slept on the ground.

A boy named Hero was clubbed in the face.

He really was named Hero.

See this penny? Where better than the train tracks?

See this dollar? Paint my face.

Your suits, ties, red faces & fatty deposits clogging aortas.

I have been watching your passionless occupation for decades

& have been plotting a shallow sex with you,

a way to eradicate your mistakes.

Forgiveness likes to pose as the sky, but

we're no known error.

It sounds & feels like change.

It sounds & feels like your number.

It sounds. It feels.

Simply quietly astonished with flawless impeccable etc.

We had a really great friendship.

PRINCE FEARLESS

You multiply, you cannot be found.
You exist without us, like irony.
Why are you annoyed?
A dimension, an air we share, the story
of a dream within a dream within a mirror –
We read it last night & went to bed snowing.

I will never bake bread to console you
or lick your cheek & say
it is the Jell-O of the moon.
The invisible husk – a book looking at me.
A boy who loves his cat too much.
As you make a simple living reading stolen letters.
Summer is still being woven in this city
& there are very few camera thieves
because there are no cameras, only
phone photos of imagined night.
Everyone stops at the waterfront park
to snap a picture – then they leave
before seeing.

I'm guessing I'm just like the rest –
exhausted, in need of a break & a few
kind words to replace my cigarette addiction.

'When the scene changes,' you pronounced, 'I'll sparkle.'

The smoke billowing out of your mouth . . .

You   multiply   you   cannot   be   found

MEDITATE

The little books fill with words

& then they empty out.

All roads lead to this.

A friend lends a love book.

Nothing is wasted here.

I'm just going to go back there & say that I failed.

Poured into a vessel

I couldn't hear anything

but water – birth sounds.

All the mothers were calling,

coins turning to gold water

dripping from their fingers.

'We have given up.'

'What?' I called. 'What?'

'We have given it all up, & now, after … '

Hollow as dollar bills strewn across the forest floor.

The mothers chanting in a tent

sewn of old money, more notes to stoke the fire …

The mothers burned all night & when they went out

the ashes whispered.

Enough teaching for now.

I didn't loan; I gave.

The light glowing mystically around the ruby & sapphire bottles
  behind the bar.

The song growling.

It wasn't simple or complicated in cafés

where our feet were always cold.

It wasn't the lone donkey in the field

or the trace of things to heal.

She has no idea how we got so strong.

How we came to rent a houseboat.

& what kind of boats we are.

Rotting, with tremendous intelligence & sensitivity.

Burning with slips of fortune paper.

Gathering the sounds, hoping the audience isn't allergic to this movie.

Our friends in jail. Taking bags of soil on the train.

We do thank copy machines & computers.

We do kiss house plants.

The skill of tolerating emotional pain,

not expecting a means or an end.

Upstairs at my sister's house,

peers' questions & a sacred place to shine our shoes.

Some call it praying & some call it wrestling.

Battling the wealth-parents –

What was it you thought you wanted?

What was it you thought you had to defend?

Your father is dead.

On the streets of L.A.

On a train to Texas.

Your father in Winnipeg, blackflies & snow.

We buzz inside frozen banks.

After it collapses: no whimpering, just work.

Melt the money: new jewellery.

Dog walking traded for fresh mint or child care.

Frame the house, dig a basement –

plants pattern the walls.

Can you believe we used to fly on planes?

(Shaking head): I once crossed the sea this way.

Walking through overgrown neighbourhoods with a friend –

We see the first monarch perched on lilac.

We go on arguing, to see what it reveals.

It's disrespectful to expect too little of us.

To shield us from new experiences.

Someone had to smash the glass & pick the ripe apples.

We see a couch with a *free* – not a *broken* – sign & sit down.

A music is beginning, just under my ribs.

My friend thinks she can face the sound.

With the blackberries before us.

THE WILD INSTRUMENTS

Hush. Broomwash.

You have spoken too soon.

The color is grey.

An outdoor day.

I snort when I laugh & I'm laughing now.

Just as you may chortle in chorus.

Missing us, our pots & pans & conviction.

There are so many kinds of bells

but we know the rusted ones are the most beautiful.

As we step up to the music school.

Enroll in an intuition class.

No tuition. Still, this education isn't free enough.

No silence & not the right kind of talking.

When you took my hand in the street,

I knew we were going to jump.

The riot-geared weren't quite ready,

their paper suits dissolving into puddles.

We can finally see them

in our unbroken reflection.

FEAR IS NOT A BODY PART

A secret cowardly message

What you are working on

If you are a scholar you

You breathe this

& if you are becoming you

You get so sick of these clothes

I'm not sure about your story – so much hurt in it.

He was just a man sitting under a tree & then

he realized something.

He's you, right? And he is she as well.

My nephew gathers stones from the shallow river

& arranges them on my windowsill.

You're rooming with normalheads now – I'm one of them,

writing bad poems & plotting a new microbrew.

See, we all babysit this baby. Let's call him Oliver. Felix. Autumn.

Sheahan. Let's call her Misca, Terrwyn, Jill.

Shrugging off these oppressive structures – easy

as changing a diaper.

We all soak beans overnight, right?

We've all meditated in a shopping mall.

It's a hot day & the water's boiling.

Let's cook these beans. Let's feast.

THE HOUSE OF GOOD & BAD

The ego identifies with a broom, a plant, a coffee maker & then me.

& I'm good. I've been good all my life. I was born good.

Except when I'm evil. Womb-evil.

Except for when I claw my way through.

Some call it consciousness. I'd rather be knocked out.

I lit a candle & the next thing I knew I was burning.

We give ourselves permission.

There's a tendency.

I'll admit to very few practices.

What we create over breakfast.

Valentine's flowers – dried – taped to the front door.

There is deserving & undeserving love (they say).

But I'm good. You know that.

Just as a separative intelligence glances – just glances – our way.

We understand the stupid milk & the goodwill.
But do we?

The aspirant gets tired of nudity & finds a new robe.

The wind in the room of the mind – birds make the wind.

A feeling both familiar & alien –

I have mentioned this before.

Have you seen it?

The house is rotting.

A TRUTH HEARING IN YOUR CITY

Even in the afterlife, it's school.

For keeping all the joys

& intense suffering.

No, we can't feel happy in a car

& there's no pure water anywhere.

Just a few of us won't die from cancer.

From concern.

You are calling yourself *brilliant, crazy* & other

adjectives we are so sick of.

This is a horrible setting for the story,

swampy with flies & mosquitoes,

the laundry music & all the lists we shouldn't have imagined.

Who is the audience, who is presenting,

who is dead & who is home sleeping?

You want to dissolve or absolve: impossible.

Look back for a long time

until you understand as fully as you possibly can.

Then take off your robes.

Learning is not enough, friend.

Now we must begin to practice.

We must do it differently this time.

NOTES AND ACKNOWLEDGEMENTS

I take it as a given that all writing is intertextual and it would be impossible for me to trace all the references and allusions in these poems, as many I am not consciously aware of. Those I know of are noted here.

Epigraph from Brian Walker's *Hua Hu Ching: The Unknown Teachings of Lao Tzu*.

'The Conditions': quote from Meher Baba's *Discourses*.

'In the Village or Pray Alone': title is a riff on Rumi's 'When We Pray Alone' in Coleman Barks's *The Essential Rumi*.

'We Are the 100%': I know that 'impossible sometimes' comes from a Jean Valentine poem; I'll be damned if I can find the poem, though!

'The Real': the first two lines riff on language from Jacob Needleman's introduction to the *Tao Te Ching* (translated by Gia-Fu Feng and Jane English).

'My Prison Studies' uses language from Martin Luther King Jr.'s 'Letter From a Birmingham Jail.'

'Feathers & Blood': 'The task for spiritual workers now' is from Meher Baba's *Discourses*. The I Ching quote is from Stephen Karcher's *The Elements of the I Ching*.

'The Art of Looking Out the Window': title from Dan Currin.

'The Art of the Spiritual Headache': 'Anarchist choir' is from the creative hearing of Susan Steudel. The poem originally read 'atheist choir,' from a conversation with Jay Starnes.

'Prince Fearless': title from Sidria Hawkins.

'The Future of Music': the title is from John Cage's essay of the same name and borrows some language from his essays on experimental music. The first line is a riff on a line from Lee Williams's 'Night Terrors.'

To any other sources I have borrowed from, my gratitude.

o

Thanks to my students and colleagues at VCC Kwantlen, and SFU's The Writer's Studio for kindnesses and learning.

Thank you to the B.C. Arts Council for a grant which gave me time to work on this book.

Thank you to Alana Wilcox, Jeramy Dodds, Evan Munday, Leigh Nash and all of the other folks at Coach House for their work on this book.

Much gratitude to Claudia Keelan and Wayne Koestenbaum for their poetry and for the blurbs.

Thanks to Meredith and Peter Quartermain of Nomados Press for publishing the chapbook *The Ends*.

Thank you to the following publications, in which some of these poems first appeared: *Alive at the Center: Contemporary Poems from the Pacific Northwest*, EVENT, *Forcefield: 77 Women Poets of British Columbia*, *The Maynard*, *Poetry Is Dead*, PRISM international, subTerrain.

Thank you to Sarah Leavitt for her awesome visual rendering/ translation of 'One Virtue' in *Poetry Is Dead*.

Thank you to Emmett Race for photos and friendship.

Gratitude to writer friends near and far, too many to name but I will name a few here: Kim Minkus and Brook Houglum (Spoon Project for life!), Raoul Fernandes, Thea Kuticka, Michael Guerra, Don Mee Choi, Jennifer Chapis, Jennifer Rabin, Emilie O'Brien, Meliz Ergin, Helen Kuk, Rachel Rose, Jordan Scott, Nikki Reimer, Jonathan Wilke, Broc Rossell, Lissa Wolsak, Renee Saklikar, Bonnie Nish, all of the amazing women of Rhizomatics, the Enpipe Line crew.

With love and gratitude for conversations on allyship and utopias: Mercedes Eng, Che Nolan, Siobhan Sloane-Seale, Christine Leclerc, Cara Cibener, Susan Steudel.

More soul-family: Lyndsay Moffatt, Josha MacNab, Sam Talbot, Monica Hepburn, Mutya Macatumpaq, Monica Weitzer, Maria Jackman.

Thank you to my mother for teaching me to read and teaching that creativity matters.

My beautiful family: Your love gives me courage. Dan, Virginia and Jane: so much gratitude for your music, which holds me.

If your name is not listed here and you think it should be: it should be. Pardon my oversight. I am hugging you now and whispering *thank you* in your ear. Thank you.

Jen Currin's previous books are *The Sleep of Four Cities*, *Hagiography* and *The Inquisition Yours*, which was a finalist for three awards and won the 2011 Audre Lorde Award for Lesbian Poetry. She lives in Vancouver and teaches at Vancouver Community College and Kwantlen Polytechnic University.

Typeset in Albertan.

Albertan was designed by the late Jim Rimmer of New Westminster, B.C,
in 1982. He drew and cut the type in metal at the 16pt size in roman only;
it was intended for use only at his Pie Tree Press. He drew the italic in
1985, designing it with a narrow fit and a very slight incline, and created a
digital version. The family was completed in 2005 when Rimmer redrew
the bold weight and called it Albertan Black. The letterforms of this type
family have an old-style character, with Rimmer's own calligraphic hand
in evidence, especially in the italic.

Printed at the old Coach House on bpNichol Lane in Toronto, Ontario,
on Zephyr Antique Laid paper, which was manufactured, acid-free, in
Saint-Jérôme, Quebec, from second-growth forests. This book was printed
with vegetable-based ink on a 1965 Heidelberg KORD offset litho press. Its
pages were folded on a Baumfolder, gathered by hand, bound on a Sulby
Auto-Minabinda and trimmed on a Polar single-knife cutter.

Edited by Jeramy Dodds
Designed by Leigh Nash
Cover design by Christine Leclerc and Leigh Nash
Author photo by Sarah Race Photography

Coach House Books
80 bpNichol Lane
Toronto ON M5S 3J4
Canada

416 979 2217
800 367 6360

mail@chbooks.com
www.chbooks.com